North Norfolk
Summer Sketchbook

James McCallum

Silver Brant

© James McCallum 2003

Published by Silver Brant
Corner Cottage
Jolly Sailor Yard
Wells-next-the-Sea
Norfolk
NR23 1LB

www.jamesmccallum.co.uk

ISBN 0-9541695-2-2

Designed by John Walters
www.johnwalters.co.uk

Printed by Healeys Printers
Ipswich 01473 461122

North Norfolk
Summer Sketchbook

James McCallum

Silver Brant

Bar-tailed godwits and sanderling with resident oystercatchers. Some of these returning waders are frequently in full breeding dress and there are few more handsome than male bartails. Wells Harbour – 5 August 2002.

Foreword

A few places grab you and never let you go. For me, first paradise was north-east Norfolk. The 'silver darlings' or herring swimming offshore gave my family a living in the week. The Broads and the great arc of coastline offered us near wildernesses at the weekend. As a wee lad, just before the war, I loved 'the beach' and its endless ribbon of pale greens and ochres, seamlessly joined to an infinite horizon between stippled sea and tall sky. Its few people were romantic characters like long-line fishermen and wildfowlers... first heroes.

Over my next itinerant 65 years I have felt all sorts of envy for those whose fates allowed them to enjoy Norfolk as their home. Not least Richard Richardson, of Cley whose observation and companionship secured for some mutual London friends a succession of wonderful encounters with good birds. My teeth still clench at the thought of the Sea Eagle that flew in during a sea-watch.

Lately I have worried that the Norfolk coast has become a bit tamer, with reserve after reserve where once we ranged free except for the odd irate keeper. My vision of paradise began to fragment and I broke my promise to myself of "one Norfolk day every year". Would, could anyone recapture, reconvene the magic?

Just sometimes, cometh the need, cometh the man. He is James McCallum of Wells. His heart is young and beats afresh to the ancient rhythm of Norfolk's natural year.

The astonishing immediacy of his 'eye-mind-hand' perception stems from best practice. He looks, sees, draws and paints only in the field.

Hence a flood of sublime, original images, not just of individual birds but also of them and other non-human beings jostling in the moments from their lives. His lyrical scenes prove that the magic is still there.

Outside in all weathers, all day long, James has nevertheless committed himself to passing on his perceptions in a series of delightful books. Their texts place his paintings in full complement of habitat and season. *North Norfolk Summer Sketchbook* is the third, being a delightful wander through marsh and heath. It takes you 'up close and personal' to mysterious creatures like Bitterns and Adders. I just love it.

And, when you've read it, don't put it on a shelf; keep it on your bedside table for better dreams.

Ian Wallace
September 2003

Barn owl hunting the highest reaches of the saltmarsh in the low sunshine of a winter's evening. Warham Greens – 14 March 2003

Introduction

The North Norfolk coast and adjoining farmland form a strip of gently undulating landscape bordered by the North Sea and crowned by unbroken sweeps of constantly changing skies. The sky is perhaps the most dominant feature of the landscape as there are no mountain ranges, crags, gorges or other prominent geographical or man-made features to interrupt the smooth horizon and form a focus point for the eye.

The sky, through its effect on the landscape, has its own special qualities; sometimes it can be dark and dramatic with huge masses of building cloud formations. At other times it can be bright, colourful and crystal clear, then cold, wild and windswept. Yet again it can be dull, grey and oppressive or still and misty. The list of combinations is endless. This is one of the appeals of this part of the east coast. It is a place of atmospheres, moods and feelings. Some people have a feel for it, while others don't, finding it flat, dull and quite boring. Many like the summer and find the winter too cold and bleak and so on. This is the way it should be. They say that there is no accounting for taste; personally I like it all year round.

There is however more to North Norfolk than just wide-open skies and landscape. A closer look at the landscape reveals, within the seemingly constant skyline, an incredibly rich and complex mix of subtly changing habitats, whose boundaries and divisions merge beautifully into each other. Sandy beaches blur to mudflats, mudflats to saltmarsh and saltmarsh to sand dunes, dunes to grazing marshes, then to cultivated fields and so on. The transition is smooth, however, and the number and variety of species dramatic. This is particularly true of the bird life and the area is rightly famous for it. Indeed many of the coastal towns and villages are famous place names in the bird world.

The marshes of Cley and its surrounding area are particularly well known and the area is sometimes referred to as the birdwatchers' Mecca. Equally rich are the grazing marshes and sandy coastline of Holkham. The coastal trees and scrub of Wells Woods have a long history of spectacular arrivals of autumn migrants. More recent developments include the creation of the reserve at Titchwell. With its wide range of habitats, freshwater pools and scrapes, reedbed, brackish marsh and saltmarshes it has become a very valuable reserve. Its attractiveness to waders and wildfowl has even begun to rival Cley marsh.

I have further, stronger ties to the area. My families on both sides originated from the coastal community here and have strong traditional connections involving the sea and coast.

I was born in Wells and grew up here and developed a strong interest in natural history, particularly birds, and later in painting. I continue to live in the area but have also spent long periods studying birds and wildlife in many other parts of the country and abroad. It is however here in Norfolk that I feel most at home and where my observations are sharpest and most instinctive.

This third book of paintings and observations of North Norfolk wildlife is intended to be different from the previous two. The first gave a basic flavour of a typical North Norfolk year in the form of a monthly introduction with associated paintings and sketches. The second, *Wild Goose Winter - observations of geese in North Norfolk* is, as the sub-heading suggests, a more detailed account of the spectacular numbers and impressive variety of geese that grace our winter landscape. Its paintings, illustrations and text were put together as a way of showing a large number of observations accumulated over many years spent outdoors watching and painting geese. I hoped that its contents would answer many frequently asked questions and provide extra information about these birds.

I wanted this new book to be less structured and to piece together paintings, sketches and writing alongside more detailed, in-depth studies in a loose, wandering manner. What I mean by this is that it can often be extremely difficult, if not impossible, to plan what you are going to be watching or painting if you choose to go outdoors and work directly from life Wildlife won't stop to pose for you or guarantee that it will be in the same place the following day.

Then it is always easy to get sidetracked or the weather can turn against you. So you have to make the best of every opportunity.

So this meandering approach, no matter how close to real life, has made the book more difficult to put together than expected. The larger chapters such as *Bitterns, Summer on the grazing marshes, Nightjars* and *Adders* represent detailed, more intimate studies made either over a period of days or weeks of intensive watching or are studies made over a complete season or several years.

This interest in behaviour and interactions increasingly appeals to me more than solely making portraits of wildlife. I've tried to link these longer chapters with pictures of other species made during the period of time in between.

Originally, the book was to include additional longer chapters and collections of paintings such as the autumn migration of land birds, sea-watching, winter estuaries and returning geese. These combined would span an entire year. However to include them all would mean cutting down the content and detail of the larger chapters. So, instead, this book deals with the end of the winter and the early signs of spring, passing through the summer and ends with the appearance of the first returning pied flycatcher of the year. This whole period of the local wildlife calendar is brought together here under the convenient title of *North Nofolk Summer Sketchbook*. The pied flycatcher is one of the first Scandinavian drift migrants to reach our shores in early August and its arrival signifies the end of summer and first real day of autumn on the east coast bird-watching calendar.

Here its arrival signifies not only the end of summer but the end of this particular book.

bright low evening sun
strange double reflections.   20 Aug 91   Eye Pool
                                              Cley

Whilst watching the waders opposite, I observed this young pied wagtail preening on a nearby fence. The sunshine cast a strong shadow on the fence post while, the sunlight reflected from the waters' surface cast an interesting secondary shadow.

Young ruff, curlew sandpiper and dunlins, Eye Pool Cley – 30 August 2001

Barn Owls

There are few sights more beautiful than a barn owl hunting over a rough pasture, with reed-fringed dykes, in low winter sunshine. Fortunately this is a regular sight in North Norfolk as the area is one of its main strongholds within the British Isles.

During late winter and early spring it, is not unusual to regularly see several birds flying over rough grassland throughout the daylight hours. It is tempting to think that with the coming of the first few warm, sunny, spring-like days, the worst is over for barn owls, and for that matter many other wintering birds, but natural food is in fact at its scarcest at this time of the year.

The main prey of barn owls is small mammals, mainly voles, mice, young rats and shrews. The short-tailed field vole is the most important prey species. A brief basic look at the life cycle of this rodent is helpful in understanding some reasons why barn owls find successful hunting most difficult at this time of year. The voles prefer rough grassland with a good under storey of dead stems and litter, particularly those areas that are not mechanically cut or disturbed, or pastures that are only very lightly grazed. Areas of intensive agriculture would seem very unlikely to be

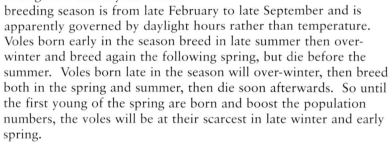

attractive to the owls; however, the untouched dyke edges and grassy field margins provide suitable breeding areas for the voles. Here they can occur in large densities and provide barn owls with long lines of excellent hunting habitat.

Short-tailed field voles live on average less than a year. Their breeding season is from late February to late September and is apparently governed by daylight hours rather than temperature. Voles born early in the season breed in late summer then over-winter and breed again the following spring, but die before the summer. Voles born late in the season will over-winter, then breed both in the spring and summer, then die soon afterwards. So until the first young of the spring are born and boost the population numbers, the voles will be at their scarcest in late winter and early spring.

This helps to explain why the barn owls are so active during the daytime at this time of year. They are to be seen hunting both on the wing and from perches such as fence posts. This latter method, although less efficient, saves their precious energy and the owls are frequently to be seen employing both tactics. Although their dark eyes have good light-gathering abilities, it is their hearing that is the main means of locating prey. The characteristic facial disc that enhances their beautiful facial expression is a specialised aid to hearing. The two halves of this facial disc channel sound to their large ear openings, which are located just inside the disc at either side of the head. The ears are asymmetrically placed so they can pinpoint noise very accurately.

Weather conditions can also be a major factor greatly affecting hunting success. Crisp, still weather is ideal as it is easy to hear small mammals moving around. Wet and windy weather, especially

when prolonged is bad for barn owls. Hearing is made difficult and their soft feathers soon become waterlogged. Prolonged heavy snowfall can also make hunting difficult, but still days with light snow are less of a problem as their excellent hearing can detect the movements of small mammals below the snow cover.

During long spells of unfavourable weather, I have picked up dead barn owls in rough grassland with no meat on their bones. Many other casualties occur on our roads as large tracts of good hunting habitat is to be found along road verges. Unfortunately this is not only a seasonal but a year-round problem.

Another more recent and worrying factor affecting the survival of barn owls in winter is the modern mania for neatness and straight lines. This human trait has crept into North Norfolk in recent decades and has seen many rough corners, path edges, sea walls, even nature reserves 'tidied up'. This clinical attitude seems to prevail and large areas of good hunting ground and wildlife pockets have disappeared, as have some of the landscape's charm and character.

Kestrels stealing food from barn owls are an additional threat to their winter survival. These falcons are after the same prey and therefore are often to be found hunting the same areas. Kestrels sit on high perches or other good vantage points. From there they will watch the owls progress. When an owl has successfully captured prey the kestrel will fly at the owl and aggressively try to steal its kill. This is to be seen most where hunting habitat is concentrated in areas or pockets such as rough meadows.

This is very energy-efficient feeding for kestrels, particularly during hard times when food is difficult to come by. Repeated attacks and robberies can put an added strain on the owls. If the falcon persists, the barn owl will have to find new hunting areas or resort to using the large linear networks of dykes and field margins where piracy is less likely.

When we are able to observe these fabulous birds so readily it soon becomes apparent that barn owls can often be different in their colours, tones and patterning. What was initially assumed to be a single regular hunting barn owl may in fact be two or more individuals. This shows that certain favoured hunting areas may be important for not just one owl but an essential part of the feeding range of many local birds. By carefully noting down and getting to know individual markings of all the barn owls you see in a local area you can build up a clearer, more intimate understanding of them. On rare occasions, particularly when the owls are having to work hard to find food, you may suddenly see all the birds and possibly an extra one, feeding over the same area at once.

This happened to me one cold evening in early March when I watched five barn owls hunting the same small, rough pasture where I had been watching one or occasionally two during the previous month.

These varying colours and markings are related to age and sex. Generally speaking, young birds are the darkest and have the highest proportion of dark peppering on the flanks. Females are generally darker than males but both sexes become increasingly pale with age. Mature males can be essentially unmarked and can appear ghostly white and really quite stunning.

A kestrel dive-bombs a barn owl that has just caught a field vole, forcing the owl to turn
over to defend itself. Now the kestrel steals the prey. Wells Beach Road – February 2000.

Barn owl hovering at the reed edge. Burnham Norton – February 2002.

Barn owl hunting voles over rough grassland. As it pounces, its sudden
appearance over a swathe of dead grasses startles a snipe and a meadow pipit. Wells Town – 25 February 2002.

Hunting from fence posts is an energy saving tactic frequently
adopted during late winter when food is scarce.
Wells Town – 14 February 2002.

14.02.02
wells Town
midday bright cold
light NE

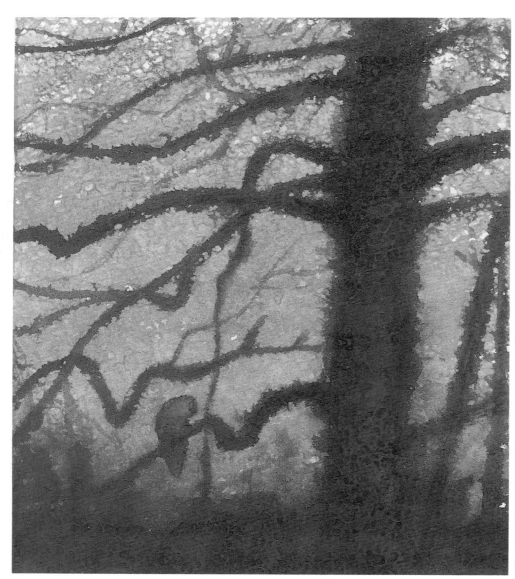

During the winter of 1997-98 I was employed to scare night feeding wigeon from winter cereal fields back onto neighbouring nature reserves. It was unusual and, at times, lonely work but the long nights, particularly moonlit ones, provided unique opportunites to gain some insight into rarely seen nocturnal activities of birds and animals. Here the distinctive sihouette of a barn owl as it stretches its head out to locate the rustling of small mammals.

Burnham Deepdale – 5 March 1998

A long-eared owl hunting the verge of a farm track in the early hours of the morning below the distinctive winter constellation of Orion.

Burnham Deepdale – March 1998

The winter draws to a close

A beautiful still evening at Wells with mist rising above the flowing tide. As the winter draws to a close many of the pinkfeet begin their journey northwards to northern England and Scotland before eventually heading off to their breeding grounds in Iceland. These will be some of the last evening flights until they return in September. March 2003.

Skylarks, twite and rock pipits feeding on pioneer saltmarsh in Holkham Bay. As the spring progresses the rock pipits begin to show signs of their summer colours. Grey heads and a pinky wash on their breasts indicate that these birds originate from Scandinavian sea coasts. Studies have shown that some of the twite wintering in Norfolk breed on the Pennines. The origin of the skylarks is less sure but very soon the muddy shore will fall silent. 6 March 2001.

16/03/99

Warm, sunny early spring days can be a good time to see the return passage of wintering raptors. Seeing a rough-legged buzzard soaring or hovering over the marshes is always a highlight, but four circling over the dunes at Wells was exceptional. 16 March 1999.

The large winter gatherings of lapwings and wigeon begin to break up and move on to more northern shores to breed.
Elements of breeding behaviour and antagonism are occasionally shown particularly on warm, sunny days. Stiffkey – February 2000.

Bittern in typical hunched posture with neck drawn in. 5 March 2002.

Bitterns

This strange and mysterious bird has only a very loose foothold as a breeding species in the region. By far the best time to encounter one is in late autumn, throughout the winter and until early spring. During this period numbers are significantly boosted by birds from overseas and occasional wanderings by British bred youngsters. Most of our wintering birds originate from populations in northern and eastern Europe.

I had first hand experience of a newly arrived immigrant on 6th November 2002 when I flushed one from the top of a seven-foot pine tree in the sand dunes to the east of Wells harbour mouth. This bird then flew high northwards, out over the beach towards the sea before turning westwards and heading off in the direction of Wells beach.

Bitterns are notoriously difficult to see well. If you are lucky you may get a fleeting glimpse of one in between the reeds or, more often than not, one flying from one area of marsh to another. If you are extremely fortunate you may have an opportunity to watch one for a long spell. This may happen purely by chance; however time and perseverance will greatly increase your chances. An important step is to recognise a potential opportunity of seeing a bittern well then act on it. For instance, if someone has watched one feeding in a specific area or I have caught a fleeting glimpse of

The bittern using its large yellow-green feet to grab reedmace stems and haul its feathered bulk through the vegetation. 6 March 2002.

one, I return to the same location several times and sit quietly and wait, hoping that this maybe a regular feeding area. Ninety-nine percent of the time it comes to nothing, but occasionally persistence pays off.

In March 2002 I had spent a couple of long, cold days waiting in vain for a bittern to appear in a marshy edge of a small coastal pool in north-west Norfolk. Earlier that week I had listened to people's accounts of it fishing for long periods and even climbing into the crown of a hawthorn to sun itself. A few days later I was chatting to another person who had seen another bittern feeding in reedmace in a marsh further along the coast. I tried to see it that same evening, then again the next day without success. It had been many years since I'd seen a bittern well and I began to feel as though I was doomed never to see another well again. A couple of days later I returned at dawn, waited for a couple of hours without a glimpse, then suddenly a bittern materialised from a wall of reedstems. It was a great moment after many near-misses and blank sheets. I watched it for a further 30-40 minutes and made some sketches. My diary for this and further successful visits reads:

4th March 2002 - still, sunny and light frost.
On my way to the marsh I pass many pheasants and partridges, with pale blue-grey patches of frost on their rumps and tails, feeding on the roadside verges. Arrive at the marsh around first light. At 8.30 am the bittern comes to the edge of an island of reeds, 35 x 30 feet in size with a couple of small, stunted sallows on the front edge. It flies clumsily to an area of dead and fallen reedmace stems at the back of the pool. Here it sits hunched until the warmth of the first rays of sun hit it. It now begins to sun itself, fluffing out the loose feathers of its crown and neck into a huge ruff. When startled by a grey heron, a female marsh harrier, a short-eared owl, a jet plane and my first ever Chinese water deer, it rapidly adopts its famous vertical camouflage posture, a peculiar sight, with neck stretched right up, now surprisingly long and thin, with its bill pointing skywards. Either side of the bill its two eyes can be clearly seen looking forwards. Later it decides to move to another area and having stretched both wings upwards it crouched then jumps up to help get airborne, flying towards a dyke full of emergent reedmace, where it crash-lands out of sight.

5th March 2002 - still, sunny start, overcast and windy by 11am
Fantastic views of the bittern for around two and a half hours. Again emerges from reed island at 8.45am. Walks through reed bed at one and a half to two feet above the waters surface. It can do this by grabbing a mass of reed stems with its huge yellow-green feet. Moves through the reeds, surprisingly fast and nimble and appears to be walking on stilts.

Bittern stretching. 5 March 2002.

A bittern's bulk is rather deceptive. They are in fact quite small, scrawny birds, their small skeleton hidden, as in owls, under a mass of thick, dense feathers. The size is further exaggerated by their large wings and characteristic huge bright yellow-green legs and feet. This relatively small body weight enables them to clamber through reeds, which appear unable to carry their bulk.

It comes to the reed edge and flops across to make a rather graceless landing in the same far corner of the pool as yesterday. Here, amongst the reedmace it fishes, frequently catching small dark objects, possibly beetles or snails and occasional frogs.

It makes progress by grabbing reedmace with its large feet and pushes its head and body through and under the large stems. It proceeds along the waterside vegetation until it comes to a small plank fence, used to stop livestock from passing around the pool edge. Comically it climbs through, then back around, then incredibly, over the fence, at this moment exposing the full reach of its long thighs, legs and feet to reach the top plank. On top it moves up the shallow angle with slow deliberate steps, back hunched, neck drawn in and bill pointing forward. All the time its body moves in a strange, slow mechanical bobbing motion. Then quite suddenly, this master of shape-changes rises up to its full height, with every part of its body at full stretch. It remains in this extreme posture for a couple of minutes, very slowly moving its head in different directions. Feeling the time is right to make a move it rocks its body in a pumping action before crouching right down to leap into flight and heads to a new area of marsh.

6th March 2002 - overcast, cool with moderate south westerly

The bittern is already out in its favourite corner when I arrive at 8.20am. Very active today in both feeding and behaviour. I watch it uninterrupted for around three and a half hours, during which time it catches two frogs, on one occasion with a water rail feeding behind it! Very active preening and wing-stretching today and during one lengthy bout of preening I witness it 'powder' itself.

Bitterns, as do herons and several other birds, possess special areas on their bodies where powder-down is produced. Powder-down comes from patches of feathers that are never moulted and grow continuously, disintegrating at their tips to produce fine powder rather like talcum powder. This is used to help clean fish and, particularly, eel slime from their plumage then also to help re-waterproof the feathers. Bitterns have two pairs positioned on the breast and flanks. When the powder has helped to dry up the slime it is removed by grooming with their feet. Furthermore on the inner edge of the long, middle toe nails are perfectly formed combs, which seem to be used to groom the feathers more thoroughly. It was fascinating to study this comb in great detail on a long dead corpse I once found at Blakeney.

Having spent many minutes delicately moving its bill through several tracts of feathers both on its body and wing it now spends several more minutes with its head under its wing, fidgeting slightly. Finally its head reappears, pale and floury, against its warm body tones. It now stands, neck drawn in and back hunched, its appearance very different now that the contrast between its dark cap and moustache has been softened by the powder. After a minute or so in this posture it becomes active once more, fluffing out its loose head and neck feathers in to a large mane, paying much attention to grooming its head and neck with its toes. Following further preening it begins to oil its feathers. Small amounts of oil from its preen gland, positioned just above the tail are secreted onto its bill or the back of its head. Now the oil can be transferred to all areas of its body and smeared onto the feathers to further waterproof them. After finishing its toilet it climbs up on to the fence once more, then, as yesterday, flies off to another area of the marsh. A very privileged insight into the life of one of our most secretive birds.

4 March 2002

21

It was interesting to note from this one species a wide range of feather functions that have evolved. These include, insulation, flight, camouflage, the production of powder-down and display (eg the ruff of head feathers that is used in threat displays). The evolution of specialised feathers that form powder-down to help clean and waterproof the other feathers of their everyday plumage is particularly interesting.

Another interesting fact that emerged from these observations and from other bitterns I subsequently managed to observe in autumn and winter is that, although often referred to as crepuscular (active in dawn and dusk) and sometimes nocturnal, all my observations of at least three different bitterns from dawn to dusk over several days suggest that they have nightime roost sites which they enter just before dusk, sometimes flying into them from afar and later emerging from them in the morning. All birds were roosting in clumps of emergent reeds surrounded by water. On several occasions birds did not emerge until an hour or more after first light. This behaviour may well, however vary from site to site and from season to season. We still have much to learn about these strange and elusive birds but keeping good accurate notes can help to build a clearer picture of some of their habits.

Bittern in camouflage posture at the edge of a reed stand. Their dense feather masses and large wing area, in common with owls, hide their scrawny bodies. A large footfull of reeds can therefore easily take their relatively light weight. None the less it is a strange sight to see one walking or running through a stand of reeds, halfway up the stems, giving the illusion of being on stilts.

6 March 2002

Still, sunny morning with the bittern pausing at the reedbed edge, halfway up the reed stems, waiting for the right moment to flop across the water to the pool edge to feed. Ripples caused by a swimming coot reflect the soft winter sunlight in regular waves up the face of the reeds and over the contours of the bitterns' body. It is also interesting to note the surprising size relationship of the two birds. 4 March 2002.

Startled by some nearby noise, the inactive bittern slowly rotates its head to check for potential danger.
5 March 2002

Although representing no threat, the sudden appearance of this hunting barn owl sees the bittern rapidly adopt its sky-pointing camouflage posture. The head and neck stripes instantly merge into the plant stems and the watchful eyes look forwards either side of the vertically angled bill. 4 March 2002.

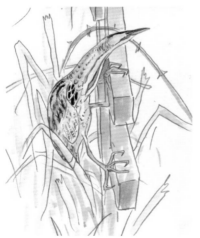

The bittern slowly made its way along the pool edge until it came to a wooden
fence used to keep livestock from passing around the muddy edges. I was
amazed to see it walk in between the planks, then clambour on to the top
where it remained for several minutes before flying to a new area to feed.
5 March 2002.

Bittern climbs through the fence, pauses on the lower strut, then comically looks back over the top strut.
3 March 2002

3ᵈ March 02

27

In early spring the male frogs acquire the dark lead breeding colours and move to open water to wait for
females to appear. After a few weeks the cycle is finished and all that remains is masses of frog spawn.
Jolly Sailor Yard, Wells – March 2001.

6 March 02, early am.
Holme Bittern catching
a frog in sheltered corner of
pool.

Taking advantage of the very vocal male frogs who had recently arrived to breed.
6 March 2002

The first signs of spring

Jolly Sailor Yard, Wells – 6 February 2000

The vocalisation of the male frogs mirrored in the bird world. Sunny evenings induce this song thrush to sing amongst the 'sticky buds' of a horse chestnut. As the spring progresses the first summer migrants begin to appear, the chiffchaff being one of the first.

A spring evening in Holkham Park, a song thrush sings from a high, draughty bough, whilst two roding woodcock weave through the canopy below. The warmer temperatures lure bats out more regularly and in higher numbers. 25 March 1999

Studies of toads on their way to dykes and marsh pools to breed.
Wells Beach, 22 March 2000

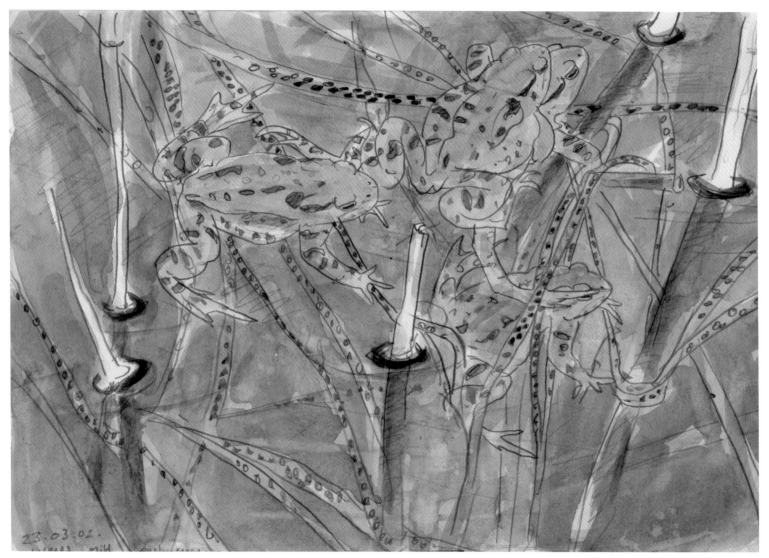

Under the water's surface male toads jostle for females and soon the underwater vegetation becomes tangled in a mass of string-like spawn.
Wells - 23 March 2002

Gregarious winter flocks of birds like bullfinches and reed buntings begin to break up into pairs and form their own breeding territories. Here a pair of bullfinches move on to the outside branches of birches as the morning sun begins to burn off the mist. Wells Beach – 22 March 2000

Pair of Reed Buntings scratching through dead stems for seeds. Gramborough Hill 12 04 01 Bright sunny but cold

A pair of reed buntings find shelter from a cold wind to sort through dead grass stems to find the seed heads.
Salthouse - 14 April 2001

Hot on the heels of the chiffchaffs, the blackcaps are amongst the first returning migrants. Their rich, clear songs fill the scrub and copses. This one sang from the crown of a dense but low hawthorn. I watched and listened to him from a gap in the canopy. Back lit, the strong sun shone through the thin skin at the base of his lower mandible, illuminating it as a fleshy orange oval. Wells Pines – 22 April 2000

Shelducks, redshanks and black-tailed godwits seen against the sun on wet mud just after the tide had gone out.
Burnham Overy – 10 April 2000

The spring is often a cross-over time for many summer and winter migrants. As masses of summer migrants pour in from their winter quarters in Africa they mix with birds that have chosen to spend their winter with us. There is no point in these shorelarks moving north just yet as the mountain and fellsides and northern shores of Scandinavia are still under thick snow and ice.

Blakeney Point – 11 April 1999

Northward bound short-eared owls may pause for a few days or
even weeks on rough grassland or set aside if the hunting is good.
Like the shorelarks their breeding ground may still be frozen.
Salthouse – 30 April 2001

In the arable land bordering the coast the resident bird populations begin to establish territories and attract mates.
A cock yellowhammer, all fluffed up, sings from a breezy hawthorn. Wells – 18 April 2002

13.04.00 Warham _____ _____ _____ still sunny just before rain

A pair of pheasants and a hare in a cereal crop. Territorial male pheasants announce their presence by puffing out their body features, expanding the fleshy wattles on their face then, throwing their heads back and calling. The display is completed with a rapid wing flutter. Warham – 13 April 2000

Springtime Adders

The adder, or viper as it is sometimes referred to, is the commonest snake to be found in this country and by far the most numerous in this region. It is our only venomous snake and is best recognised by its dark zigzag marking running the whole length of the back. It is a small snake, mature adults ranging from around one and a half to two feet in length. It is usually very timid by nature preferring to slide away into cover or into holes when approached.

Many people are frightened by adders and they have long been surrounded by superstition. Cases of people being bitten by adders are very rare and even more rarely fatal. Treated with respect you would be very unlikely to receive a bite. However, some people when aware of their presence will still actively seek them out and destroy them so I remain secretive and protective of the areas that I regularly watch, even to the extent of carrying a flower or insect book with me so that if people ask what I'm doing I tell them that I'm trying to identify plants or insects.

The name adder originally comes from the Anglo Saxon *naedre*, later referred to in Middle English as *nedder* or *nadder*, evolving into today's familiar name.

Over several days the male's eyes turn from copper to opaque grey, then copper once more. This shows that its skin is loose and shedding is imminent.

The beginnings of a study

On the first warm, sunny day of spring the air is full of bird song: skylarks overhead, song thrushes, robins and blackbirds in gardens and copses while others like dunnocks, wrens and chaffinches sing from the thorn hedges nearby. Even a few small tortoiseshell and peacock butterflies may be coaxed out of hibernation by the sun's warm rays.

For many years I had made a promise to myself to visit heathland during such days to look for basking adders. I hadn't seen any for some years and was keen to draw them. But always up to now the sudden burst of spring warmth and activity would side-track my thoughts and I'd ended up watching and drawing courting pheasants and partridges or some other springtime bird displays. Then the first returning migrants would begin to appear and by the time I remembered the adders it would all be too late.

One springtime my memory was jogged by my mother who had seen several adders during a walk with her two dogs. She had noted several basking and others moving along narrow paths and through rabbit runs, and had remarked how they really unnerved one of the dogs. I returned to the area and managed to see several briefly basking, but it was then too late in the season for they were very active and frequently on the move. Nevertheless I found this re-introduction to adders exciting and after such a long time, it was like seeing something new for the first time.

A moving adder startles a great tit.

The snakes had made such an impression on me that the following spring I didn't forget to search for them. On the first warm, sunny day I returned to the same place and looked long and hard for them but, frustratingly, could not find any there and only found occasional individuals during searches of further areas. In the meantime, a couple of friends had found an excellent site, where it was very easy to observe adders. After several days of watching, sketching and note-taking during the following weeks, a pattern began to emerge. The snakes' behaviour, when pieced together, showed a fascinating and engrossing sequence of events and formed the basic pattern of their springtime activities. These first season's findings fitted in well with previously published material and it appeared that the long hours of observation had been rewarded with much insight into rarely-seen behaviour. These original notes and drawings could be double-checked and fine-tuned during subsequent springs and firmer dates recorded and more detail of the behaviour of the vipers in this part of the country established.

Adder on the move.

Hibernation

From late October until they emerge in early spring, adders hibernate underground in holes and burrows. These areas can be used year after year and become traditional hibernating dens. Once you become familiar with them, these are the best places to check in early spring for the first emerging snakes. In late summer I have seen adders, smooth and great crested newts and common and natterjack toads resting together under dead logs and old pieces of tin suggesting that these species may all share the same hibernating den.

Emergence and early spring behaviour

Cold-blooded reptiles basking in the first rays of warm sun are a feature of early spring. Adders can be seen sunning themselves from February onwards. However they are not usually seen out basking regularly, in any numbers, until the middle of March. Males are the first to emerge and it is not unusual to see small groups curled up together. The females put in their first appearances two or three weeks later, often only being seen regularly towards the end of March. The best areas to see them are heathland or sandy commons, which are exposed to direct sun.

The following paragraphs and sections have been interspersed with diary extracts in order to give a fuller idea of the experience of watching snakes in the field and how a basic understanding of the snake's behaviour is achieved. The observations and paintings are made through binoculars mounted on a tripod, which enables close observation without disturbing the timid adders and allows free, natural behaviour.

27th March 2002 - hazy sunshine, warm out of the cold east wind. Lots of males begin to emerge now, including my biggest ever group to date of eight curled up in a heap together. Others are dotted around in further sheltered spots, mainly singles or twos together. The males are quite dull and marked with browns and greys. Several have opaque, pale grey eyes looking 'blind'.

Opaque eyes are the first indications that the males are ready to shed their skins.

Three males curled up sunning themselves. Their opaque grey-glazed eyes show that they are ready to moult into their breeding colours.
28 March 2002

Skin shedding

Adders may shed their skins several times a year. The mature males will shed theirs first, soon after emerging towards the end of March, in readiness for the breeding season. Snakes ready to shed are obvious in their lack of bright colour and contrast, but most particularly in the cloudy or opaque look of their eyes. This is due to the separating from the eye of its transparent cover known as the brille. However, a day or several days before shedding, the eye will become clear and copper-coloured once more. This indicates that the old brille is free from the new skin.

When I first encountered males with opaque eyes I was sure that they were ready to shed their skins so I concentrated on them for a couple of days eager to see the event but was initially somewhat puzzled when the eyes turned copper again.

Shedding begins with the skin becoming detached from the lips; from here the snake pushes its head and body against vegetation to free the old skin. As it moves forwards the old skin is snagged and becomes turned inside out as the snake frees itself.
Observations in captivity have shown this process taking hours or even days, the shed skin being broken and fragmented in the process. My own observations (or lack of observations due to unlucky timing!) show that this process can take minutes only and the shed skins are frequently found totally intact, or, if not, with one or two small tears only. So, shedding seems to be easy for these wild adders and the process may happen very swiftly.
In the last week of March 2002 I saw several male adders in various stages of cloudy eyes or copper eyes. I began to visit them daily and having established where each male was, I decided to visit them in a regular circuit. On the last day of the month my diary reads:

31st March 2002 - newly-shed male adder in full breeding colours. A lovely pale lime green with blackish zigzag. The eyes bright and shiny, deep copper-coloured and the newly exposed scales have a velvety sheen to them.

A male adder that has just moulted is a very handsome creature. The newly shed skin, still fully intact, was turned inside out during the process. Note the flattened posture of the upper half of its body, where the adder has exposed as much surface area as possible to the warm rays of the sun. 1 April 2002

1st April 2002 - *hazy sun with cloudy spells.*
Spent the day watching again, one snake has already shed when I arrive. First two females out today and the males becoming more active and mobile.

2nd April 2002 - *hazy sun with dull cold periods. Moderate south wind. Continue regular circuit of male adders, becoming a little disillusioned. Then see four males curled up together with heads all facing the same way decide to make a painting, as they look great. I finish the painting and make another circuit. The first adder I come to is sitting as bold as brass in full breeding splendour next to his cast skin. Panicking I run around to the next male to find the same scenario, then to another shed male. I can't believe that after all these days waiting, this one painting cost me the spectacle of an adder shedding its skin in the wild. I feel totally deflated and really quite tired, then I see the funny side.*

Basking males becoming active, one individual picking up some scent with his flicking tongue. 28 March 2002

Adder yawning

They had all shed around three o'clock so I waited for an hour or so but the temperature was getting cooler and some of the snakes began to disappear underground. Weary but lightly amused, I headed home.

I was really determined to see an adder shed its skin. Five males had already shed and, with the emergence of at least two females, males were beginning to become more active and mobile. So, with my options reduced, I decided to change tactics and target an individual male instead.

3rd April 2002 - *warm and sunny*
Watch male basking near to a birch with distinctive double trunk. His eyes have been clear for a few days and the skin covering its scales, including the large plate-like scales on its underside has visibly separated. Occasionally I see it rubbing the sides of its head against dead bracken fronds, everytime convinced that something is about happen.

In the late afternoon I watch it 'yawning' half a dozen times, with its mouth fully open. The head and lower jaw open to produce a shape somewhere between a 'Y' and 'T' in profile, the fangs fully exposed. I'm hoping that these stretches may free the skin from the lips and begin the process of shedding.

In the hottest part of the day, 2-3pm all adders withdraw into cover and shade. The whole experience of watching is becoming very tiring, particularly when combined with the previous weeks' intense concentration.

Tired and having sat too long in the sun I find myself looking intensely through tripod-mounted binoculars at individual scales, trying to convince myself that more and more are becoming free from the old skin. The sun shining on the loose skin gives it a dull blue-grey sheen. Late afternoon becomes evening and the sun falls behind the trees bordering the heath and the adder retreats underground, its skin still not shed.

Having arrived back at the car I realised that I'd been watching the same snake for over eight hours, during which time I had seen several males moving across the immediate area, their tongues flicking rapidly, most probably picking up the scent of recently emerged females. At one stage a half-grown adder about nine inches long, probably one of last years' young, came out to bask nearby.

Watching natural history is, for me very fulfilling and enjoyable. However, times like these can be very monotonous, albeit essential if you are ever to fully understand or observe the complete life cycles of our fabulous wildlife. The following morning I knew I had to return to the same snake at the 'double birch trunk'.

4th April 2002 - *hot hazy sunshine cold easterly by late afternoon. Watch the same adder again for nearly five hours. At half past one it suddenly becomes active, after having spent the last week or so in the exact same spot. It's tongue flicks rapidly as it sets off at walking pace over a large area, along paths, then through dead bracken and thick heather and is quite difficult to keep up with at times. It is clear that I'm not going to see an adder shed its skin this year. However, following this individual might show further clues to behaviour. Could it be hunting or picking up the scent from a female? The most interesting part of this sortie is that it visits three known hibernating dens along its route and finally disappears into a hole at the last one.*

Newly emerged female. Females are usually larger and duller coloured than males. This one was beautifully marked in rich brown and yellow – a real 'tiger-striped' individual.
7 May 2001

Four males tightly coiled up together with heads all facing the same way. Making this painting cost me the sight of an adder shedding its skin!
2 April 2002

The dance of the adder - (the beginning of the mating season)
Now they have acquired their new breeding colours, the males frequently become very mobile, often being seen moving across the heath with tongues flicking. It is unclear whether these activities are to do with searches for food, following their long hibernation, or for recently emerged females, or a combination of both. One thing is certain; it will soon be the females that become the dominant focus.

Newly emerged females spend much time basking and may be joined by more than one male, but soon each female will be regularly guarded by a single male. Here the pair will lie curled up together. When the female begins to come into breeding condition the male becomes very active around her. Her condition and readiness to mate seem to be indicated by scent. The excited male flicks his tongue rapidly over the female's back, moving his body forwards following her curved and coiled shape. His movements are now performed in a curious fevered manner, jerking slightly and appearing to lightly vibrate and tremble. If the female is not ready to mate she may attempt to move to another nearby area and the male may move with her in this same trembling manner. If the male is over persistent she may move underground or into cover.

5 May 2001

The amazing spectacle of 'dancing' adders. This mesmerising display is one of my all time highlights of watching wildlife.
5 May 2001

5 May 2001

She is now obviously giving off scent, which attracts other males to her. The reaction of the guarding male to the approaching males can be incredible and frequently results in the famous 'dancing'. This was once thought to be part of the adder pair's courtship but is actually two rival males ritually fighting over a female.

My first observation of such an event stunned and amazed me. On this particular day, 4th May 2001, I watched this display on five occasions and it remains one of my most exciting and rewarding highlights of watching and recording natural history.

4th May 2001 - warm and sunny
Yesterday six adders were visible, four males and two females. The females were each guarded by a male. Lots of courtship and also mating was observed on one occasion.

Today two, sometimes three females are visible in the same area, a small clump of gorse surrounded by dead bracken and a few clumps of heather. Beneath the gorse are several old rabbit and a few rodent holes, which have become one of the adders' hibernating dens. On the sheltered sunny side the females bask, each guarded by a male, the same individuals as yesterday. As I watch and sketch, several wandering males approach this area.

The guarding male becomes tense on their approach and often pokes his head towards the rival. Sometimes this is enough and the rival moves on, this being particularly true of some of the small, less mature, males. However, on five separate occasions rivals are not put off by the defending male and this results in spectacular dances. The defending male darts out at surprising speed, both males now raise up the fore parts of their bodies, and move forwards side by side at a pace. With their bodies intertwined they make forceful attempts with their erect fore-necks to push their opponents' head to the ground. Sometimes the force is quite violent and the process continues until one gives in and breaks away to speed off with the victor in hot pursuit. On a couple of occasions the adders were so involved with the ritual that I had to walk backwards to avoid them crashing into me!

Having seen off its rival, the triumphant male returns to guard the female.

At this time the pair's courtship can be observed throughout the day. The male frequently curls the tip of his tail upward, rather reminiscent of a rattlesnake, and slowly and rhythmically waves it around.

Before mating the pairs activity intensifies and they writhe around together. This courtship may last an hour or more until the female is ready to mate. Then she will relax, mating will take place freely and the pair may mate several times during this period.
It seems that the whole breeding cycle is synchronised as with frogs and toads, for soon afterwards these areas become quiet. Males are only occasionally seen passing through and the most frequently observed basking adders are the now pregnant females.

For the final chapter in the adder's life I will have to wait, for the males are now very active and the vegetation, especially the dense understorey of bracken fronds make observation very difficult. Searches for newly-born young in August and September have so far been unsuccessful so there is still plenty more to be learnt about these fabulous reptiles.

An extremely tightly coiled male.

Summer on the Grazing Marshes

The freshwater coastal grazing marshes are one of the most characteristic habitats of the North Norfolk coastline. These are recognised by a patchwork of short turfed pastures, intersected by vast networks of ditches and bordered by miles of barbed wire fences to keep livestock in. Many ditches contain reeds or have reed edges and most areas have one or more reed beds of varying size.

These areas can be very rich in bird life, particularly waterfowl, especially large numbers of grazing wigeon in the winter months, and breeding waders, in particular lapwing and redshank, in the summer. The reed-filled ditches and reedbeds bring further specialist breeders to the list, notably marsh harriers, bearded tits, reed warblers and water rails.

The richness of these habitats doesn't happen purely by accident. The actual land itself is mainly reclaimed from the sea by man in past centuries. The majority of these areas are now managed by local and national conservation bodies and a lot of hard work goes into maximising the full potential of them, especially for breeding waders. This involves improving and maintaining the drainage system so that the water flow through the entire area can be efficiently controlled, keeping many fields wet. This is attractive to waders, and provides the birds with suitable conditions for rearing young chicks.

Species like lapwing in the summer and wigeon in the winter require short turf and this is provided by cattle grazing in spring, summer and early autumn

Marsh Harriers

Bearded Tits

and by mechanical mowing in the late autumn. These examples illustrate the basics of habitat management but the whole process is of course much more complex and varies from site to site. One major pitfall in having such rich pockets of birdlife is that the high densities of eggs and young of breeding birds become the focus for predators. These so called 'honey pots' may experience such high levels of predation that in some years almost no young will be raised. Such situations have caused a dilemma for the organisations involved but many have concluded that some level of predator control may have to be implemented if populations of these specialist birds are going to continue to thrive.

Some believe that the overall management of these areas can be likened to intensive farming for key species of birds and results in a rather regimented, characterless landscape.

It is easy to see this perspective. However, with so much pressure on much of our remaining countryside it is hard to think of a better solution. Nevertheless, some grazing marshes in north-west Norfolk have small pockets of fields and margins left less intensively managed to increase their attractiveness to a wider variety of wildlife. This produces a much more dynamic habitat and a varied and interesting landscape but consequently may attract fewer key species such as lapwing. So it is a difficult balance to strike.

Observations and regular surveys help to shed much light on the effects of management and should help to keep it developing and evolving. I've been lucky to be involved with breeding bird surveys on some of the prime locations on this coast. I always find it very fulfilling and interesting work and it is particularly

Lapwing

Displaying lapwing at Holkham Freshes. Although a familiar sight and sound of early spring and summer on the grazing marshes, these tumbling aerial displays are as spectacular as you will find anywhere in the bird world. The late evening mist giving the performance a whole new atmosphere.
25 March 2003

exciting to survey areas before and after improvements in management to see how numbers and productivity develop. I have particularly enjoyed contracts which have given me a free rein regarding methods and working times. This has the attraction of being flexible with working times, for instance spending long hours when it is still and sunny in the morning and evening. These are the most productive periods for watching bird behaviour and movements.

It is possible to treat the survey as a study-block, telling the story of the birds' summer on the grazing marshes. It is possible to record complete stories of the breeding cycle from arrival and the setting up of territories with all the songs, display flights and posturing that go with territory and attracting mates; the low profile periods during incubation until the hatching of the young, and all the drama, hope and anticipation of the first young taking to the wing. This will ultimately lead to the end of the season and subsequent migration. Then the time comes for reflection on the outcome, with all the highs and lows of that particular nesting season.

For many people with less time I would recommend making a point of visiting one of the nature reserves with easy to observe species such as lapwings and avocets. Spend a couple of hours on each visit. Watching them, you soon get your eye in and become familiar with behaviour and displays, then later seeing them incubate and so on. Take a few notes after each visit to record what is happening. It's amazing, looking back at the end of the summer, how much you have seen and learnt. With these weekly snap-shots, it is possible to see how the story of each individual pair's summer unfolded.

The spectacular aerial tumbles are only part of the lapwing's striking visual displays. A male, having made a scrape, 'tidies' the surrounding area in a ritualised manner by tossing small stones and vegetation over his shoulders.

On the approach of a female he reacts by performing a 'scraping' display. Lowering his chest into the depression he lifts and parts his closed wings and with tail slightly dipped, kicks back with his legs as if removing soil once again. The feathers of his crest are erected and frequently parted.

If the female is interested she will try out the scrape. The male, reacting to her response, steps out of the nest cup and tilts his body vertically, the rich cinnamon coloured feathers of his under tail directed towards her and fanned out to show the colour to full effect. He begins to 'tidy' the surrounding area once more in the same exaggerated manner. This behaviour may be repeated many times at this or at further scrapes. Such rituals seem to be an important part of the courtship and serve to strengthen pair bonds. The pair may mate several times during similar ceremonies and eventually the female will select one of the scrapes to nest in.

Avocets

The courtship ceremony of the avocet is beautiful to watch. One minute the pair are feeding side by side then suddenly the male begins preening and the female adopts a submissive posture.

His preening actions become more and more exaggerated. Frequently the female will turn her head away from him so he will gracefully move to the other side of her then back to the other and so on. At the height of this fevered activity he flutters upwards, his long pale blue legs come out of the water to rest on her back. With his wings held upwards the pair mate. Often after mating the pair run forward, both arcing away from each other with bills lowered. Sometimes their upward curving bill tips catch the waters' surface creating a small flash of disturbed water.

A dispute between three pairs of avocets. It is not uncommon to see similar situations when several pairs gather in noisy groups facing each other in loose arcs and make forward movements to see who will stand their ground.

Here the centre pair lose their cool and, in a mixture of flying and running, depart. This action would appear to be concerned with territory and dominance but whether it is connected with feeding or nesting territories I am not sure. Whatever the reason it is certainly entertaining to watch.

23 April 2002

High over the marshes is the high-pitched cry of a displaying male marsh harrier. Once learnt it provides the key to witnessing a dramatic aerial display. The male twisting, stooping and climbing makes wild arcs high in the clouds. Suddenly he dives, twisting and turning out of the sky until he is just above the reed bed where the female has risen to greet him. Briefly they grapple talons and disappear into the reeds together.

This dramatic show can be seen regularly over the coastal reserves and marshes, but is easily missed if you don't familiarise yourself with that high-pitched call of the male. Showers – 23 April 2001

The male performs his butterfly
display flight.

Blakeney saltmarsh – 24 April 2001

58

Redshank Courtship

Male hovers to land on female's back.

The male calling constantly begins to vibrate his wings. The wing-beats become more excited and gradually he stands taller and taller until he is on tip-toes before getting airbourne.
21 April 2002

Pair mate.

After mating the pair often run forwards calling.

Single pairs of redshank, avocet and shelduck. The male redshank reacts to another which lands nearby by raising his wings and calling. The dunlin, however, are still in flocks as these birds are en route to Siberia to breed. Arnold's Marsh – 25 April 2002

Courting marsh harriers – 23 April 2001

Sedge warblers have set up territories at regular intervals along the dyke edges. They prefer marshy areas which are interspersed with occasional bramble and hawthorns. From these thorny perches they sing their loud chattering song which is frequently combined with a jerky song flight.

3 April 2002

The marshes are now a wealth of activity. Gadwall drakes pursue a duck across the meadows while behind them is a courting pair of redshank. Wing lifting to show pale underwings is common behaviour in many wading birds and serves simply to say 'here I am'.

25 April 2001

8·4·03 . Holkham.

2♀ incubating ♂ nearing. sunny strong E. sun+easterly period drying out marshes

These lapwings are now incubating their full clutches of four eggs. The closest female guarded by her mate.
Holkham – 8 April 2003

Incubating and brooding waders have to endure all manner of weather conditions to keep their eggs and small young warm and dry. I watched this incident from the comfort of Dauke's hide at Cley. As the already torrential rain intensified this incubating avocet, in common with all the other birds on the scrape, angled its bill directly into the rain storm. This behaviour was adopted by birds as large as greylag geese and continued until the rain eased. 25 April 2001

This remarkable encounter between a male marsh harrier, female sparrowhawk and starling was observed on the fresh marsh at Blakeney. Initially I was watching the soaring harrier when suddenly it stooped at great speed. Looking through the reed edge of a drainage dyke I could see a sparrowhawk that had just caught a starling and was mantling it with its wings as it tried to kill it. The harrier was attempting to rob the hawk of its prey. The sparrowhawk now tried to make off with its meal but in all the commotion the starling managed to escape minus a few feathers and the raptors both went hungry. Blakeney Freshes – 21 April 2001

Nesting lapwings and redshanks are defensive of their nesting territories and readily team up to drive away predators. Cock pheasants, although not a threat, are for some reason, treated the same way.
Blakeney – 25 April 2001

Blakeney Freshes 10 May 01
high sun
moderate Swilly

After incubating their clutches for around four weeks the eggs begin to chip and the
young soon hatch. Within a few hours their down dries out and the young are able
to run around and feed themselves. Blakeney – 10 May 2001

Lapwings, in common with other waders, will only begin to continually incubate their eggs once a full clutch of four is laid. For a lapwing it takes around five days to lay all its eggs and by delaying the incubation the other eggs will not begin to warm. This clever tactic ensures that all the young will hatch at around the same time. In the breeding season birds develop bare patches of skin either side of the breast bone so body heat is applied directly to eggs and young. Here a female lapwing broods four small chicks who instinctively find these patches once she has crouched down and called them to her. Blakeney – 9 May 2001

Although lapwing chicks are the first to hatch, it is not long before the first avocet
and redshank young appear. Blakeney – 25 May 2001.

A pair of redshank with five to six day old young feeding on a hatch
of small flies in a small marshy hollow. These lower marshy areas of
the grazing fields are remnants of small saltmarsh creeks that have
filled with sedges and rushes. The pairs' fourth young has disappeared
deep into the vegetation and they anxiously call for it to return.
Blakeney Freshes – 26 May 2001

Over the next few weeks the young will be very vulnerable to predators. 8 May 2001

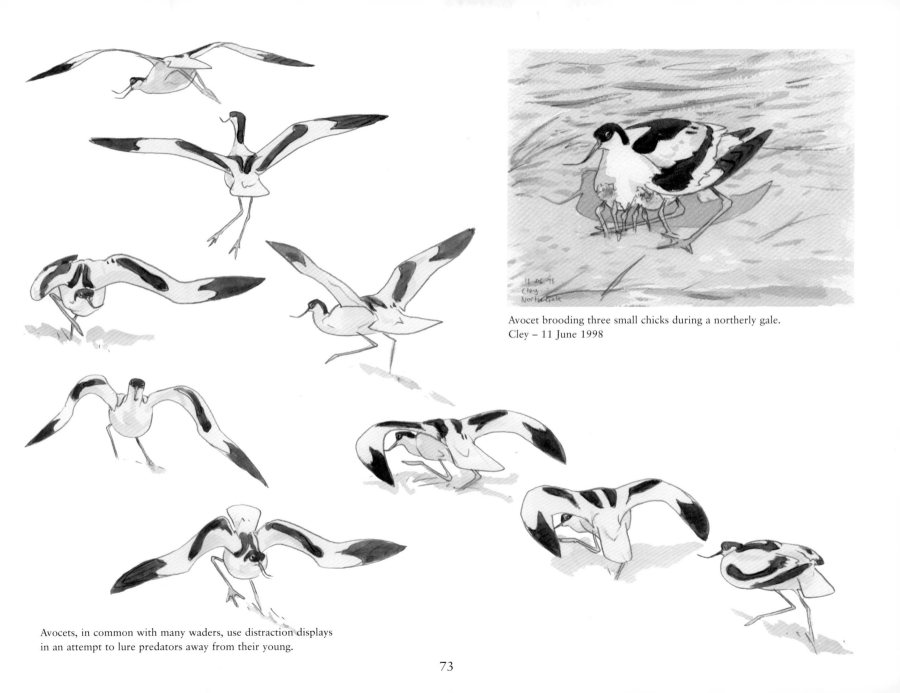

Avocet brooding three small chicks during a northerly gale.
Cley – 11 June 1998

Avocets, in common with many waders, use distraction displays
in an attempt to lure predators away from their young.

On this warm, still evening the female lets the young feed after
sunset while behind them a pair of gadwall dabble. The drake
guarding his mate until she is ready to nest.
12 May 2001

During the heat of the day one of the pair dozes. The other adult,
although actively preening, keeps an ever watchful eye out for danger.
They have already lost their other two young. 26 May 2001

75

Although often thought of as a fish eater, grey herons are one of the main predators of avocet young. The pale chicks show up well against the grass and mud and also in twilight and moonlit periods when herons are equally active. So the adults join forces and try to drive them away.

Arnold's Marsh, Cley – 29 May 2001

Some young escape the attention of predators and the long June daylight hours allow
them to feed for most of the day which enables the young to grow rapidly.
Blakeney – 2 June 2001

It is a full-time job trying to look after and protect their young. Here a redshank
calls to its 'head-strong' young as it disappears off to feed by itself.

East Bank, Cley – 31 May 2001

In the small towns and villages that border the marshes starlings are busy feeding young.
The male, told by his dark iris and bluish bill base, brings in a small grub.
Jolly Sailor Yard, Wells – 18 May 2001

When fledged the starlings (here a female with pale iris and a plain bill) take their young to the marshes where food is readily available. It is an interesting contrast between the noisy families of starlings who still depend on their parents to feed them and the redshanks' young who, under the protection of their parents, are able to feed themselves as soon as they can walk. East Bank, Cley – 23 May 2001

As the young avocets develop, hints of more adult-like plumage begins to grow and replace the pale grey down.
Blakeney – 2 June 2001

Midday sunny + humid 2 young sleep adult resting beside.

Dozing young watched over by a resting parent, its ever watchful eye looking for potential danger. Compare the same young on page 70 only 18 days before this.
Midday, hot and humid, Blakeney Freshes – 12 June 2001

humid inactive preening
12 June 01
Blakeney Freshes

Before commencing feeding once more the young, resting on
their boney ankle joints, begin to preen. 12 June 2001

Redshank, lapwing and avocet join forces to drive away another grey heron.
9 June 2001

9 June 01 Blakeney Freshes
midday cold NW rain showers.

14·06l·01 Blakeney Freshes
first fledged young of season

After all the trials and tribulations it is a great moment when the first
young waders are able to take to the wing. Here an anxious lapwing
calls to its recently fledged young, complete with tiny crest and neat
pale-edged feathers on its back. Blakeney –14 June 2001

Town Owls

It is interesting how simple chance circumstances can develop into periods of intensive drawing or study.

The following observations of tawny owls made over a couple of days is a perfect example. I had popped into my family home at Wells as I frequently do when in the town. As I was leaving, one of my brothers was coming in so we had a few words. Just before we said our goodbyes he casually remarked "Oh there's some young owls at the top of the road." He is not much interested in wildlife and I must admit I was initially a little taken aback, then took a short walk to investigate. 'The top of the road' is in fact where a section of pavement runs parallel to the south edge of a small mature wood bordered by tall wooden fences and a brick and flint wall.

Fortunately many of the larger trees here have preservation orders on them and their welfare had been closely monitored over the

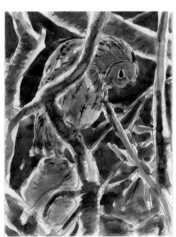

years by some of the older local residents. So far this has saved them from the fate of other woods and large gardens in the town that have been replaced by modern housing. These pockets of trees have become increasingly important lifelines for nesting birds and insect communities. This particular wood even more so as its current owners leave it mainly undisturbed. This makes it very attractive to tawny owls and, although they nest here most years, they are very difficult to observe. This year, however, was different.

As I got to the top of the road I could immediately see one youngster, then another, both sitting on bare open boughs just 20 feet above the pavement. These owlets had not long left the nest as they were still quite small and mainly clad in pale grey down, with only the stumpy beginnings of wing and tail feathers protruding from their sheaths. They were both quite mobile, actively clambering about the branches, while deeper in the wood a tense-looking parent was watching anxiously. The smaller of the two owlets was now moving towards a cluster of twigs and dead leaves, woven into a mass of dead ivy stems placed between a large tree fork. Here was a further youngster, smaller still; this was the nest site, an old collapsed squirrel's drey. It was remarkably close to the path and relatively unobscured by foliage. Many people, including myself, must have walked right underneath this nest while the female incubated her eggs, then later her small young continuously for over a month. During this time she will have been fed by her mate under the cover of darkness or in the very early morning.

It was a warm, sunny evening and a lot of people were out and about so I decided to leave, so as not to draw attention to the owls. My return at first light the following morning gave me several hours in which to watch and draw. I sat on the pavement on the opposite side of the road watching through a telescope. It was a beautiful still, sunny morning, cold at

In the late evening the owlets begin to call incessantly and the first bats start to emerge.
One of the old owls tries to work out what is watching them from the shadows below.
It bobs its head from side to side in an attempt to see past the v-shaped bow, unhappy
with the result it cranes its head around the branch to get a clearer view.
22 May 2001

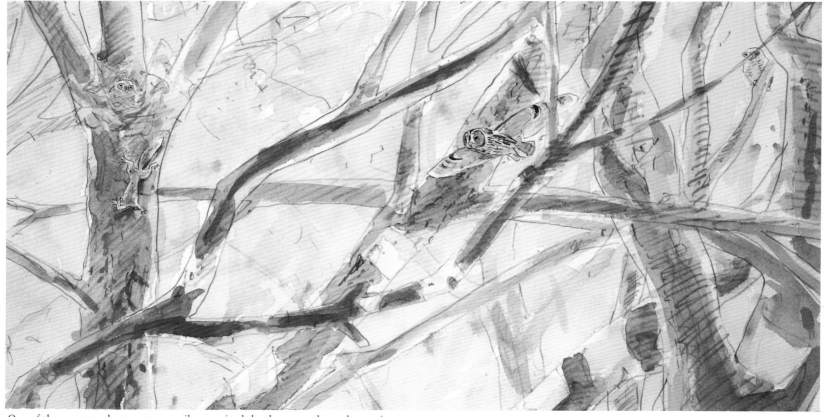

One of the parent owls attempts to strike a squirrel that has strayed too close to its young.

first until the first warm rays burst over the pantiles. It was an incredibly different place at this time of day, without the noise and movement of people and cars, just a brief but rich dawn chorus and the food-begging hisses and antics of the owlets.

It was amazing to watch the adults behaving freely in the crisp full light of early morning, unaffected by my presence. They were very alert, listening and looking around and below for rodents and birds. I saw one swoop down several times, returning with young rats, a wood mouse and a 'flopper' starling.

After a couple of days, all three young had moved deeper into the wood. It was possible to hear them but only occasionally to see them.

Whether the young chose to move there or the adults called them or lured them there with food is not totally clear, although the latter seemed more likely. This idea was strengthened by the observation of one adult landing next to an owlet with prey, then while the owl begged to be fed, the parent moved back a few branches to the next tree. This was repeated a couple more times and indeed the young did begin to clamber towards the parent with food.

Tawny owls are very protective of their young and if they feel that the owlets are in real danger they will readily attack potential enemies, including man. The parents' defensive attitude towards their young was dramatically illustrated on the second morning. I could see the smallest young sitting alone in its squirrel-drey nest, while directly behind, several trees back, was an adult, probably

Owl with young rat

the female, watching me. I began to draw the parent, when suddenly it became really tense, drawing its feathers in tightly and bobbing its head from side to side. Then I realised that a squirrel was making rapid progress towards the nest. As it approached the nest, the adult owl launched its attack, flying direct, hard and fast and I could see that it was intending to kill it. At the last minute the squirrel saw the owl and fled down the trunk at full speed and was lucky to escape.

As the family moved deeper into the wood and became more difficult to see I realised just how lucky I had been to encounter it in such an easy to watch location; particularly in that small window between the young leaving the nest and moving into deeper cover. All this resulted from a casual remark from my brother only two and a half days before.

Having spent an early morning watching the 'town owls' I decided to have a walk through Wells Pines. Walking through the first kissing gate I could hear a commotion caused by the alarm and mobbing calls of small birds. It seemed that I couldn't get away from tawny owls that week, for the local birds had found another in the birches. The bird-rich birch and bramble scrub held good numbers and variety of species. This owl had a good supporting cast of blackbird, chaffinch, bullfinch, redpoll, goldcrest and two blackcaps mobbing it.

89

Nightjars

To stand quietly alone at dusk on a clear, still evening watching and listening to nightjars is a wonderful, almost magical, experience. I'm attracted by birds such as nightjars that are shrouded in mystery and woven into folklore. To learn about them and study them is challenging and you may have to develop a whole new approach to observation and recording.

In the late spring and early summer of 2001 I spent a lot of time sitting quietly observing and sketching the antics of nightjars in a quiet corner of a local heath. There had been a lot of long overdue management over large areas of this heath to clear some of the invading scrub and prevent pockets of heather from being smothered. This work would help the area flourish as a heath rather than develop into woodland and therefore help the specialist natural history that lives on it.

In my chosen corner a large rectangle of ground had been cleared, and the area divided into two by a long pile of debris comprising mainly mature gorse and small birches. At regular intervals prominent branches or dramatically twisted roots protruded from the pile and several of these were to become favoured perches of churring male nightjars. I began to make visits both at dawn and dusk making drawings and taking notes. Sitting silently and unobtrusively I began to interpret and understand the meaning of certain calls and behaviour. Early on it became clear that there were several territories around the area and the behaviour of the females indicated that they had already begun to nest. To my amazement two of the females appeared to favour areas right next to the path leading from the car park to the clearing, frequented by myself, dog walkers and other people using the heath. I had expected that they would prefer some less disturbed areas in which to nest, which were inaccessible to people.

So, having identified the possible locations during my earlier dawn and dusk visits I paid extra attention one morning as I moved along the path back to the car. Incredibly I could see both female

A male nightjar glides by on silent wings, his white wing and tail spots show up well in the twilight. The silence only broken by his abrupt 'churrib' call. 10 June 2001

6 June 01 ...

An incubating female sits tight on her nest on the bare open ground. She is superbly
camouflaged against the background of dead gorse and bracken. 6 June 2001

nightjars sitting very close to the path. Both were sitting tight with their eyes almost closed in order to conceal the their large, black eyes with their bright eye-catching, shining highlights. Now their cryptic markings were working at their best and I was surprised that I managed to notice them at all. Although surprised and excited I had to keep my composure and pretend that I hadn't seen them for if I had stopped dead and looked the birds would have known that their camouflage had not worked and this would surely unnerve and certainly disturb them.

Instead I carried on walking and averted my gaze. I noted a couple of field marks, which could be lined up from a much greater and safer distance, so that the birds could be looked at through a telescope without disturbance.

Even so, finding them again was considerably harder than I'd ever imagined. The dead stems and fragments of gorse, warmer tones of old bracken fronds all forming a complex tapestry intersected by an equally complex pattern of shadows. These tones and patterns were perfectly mirrored in the plumage of the sitting nightjar. I found it incredible that a bird the size of a slender blackbird could vanish into a square metre of relatively flat heathland. The solid form was counteracted by clever patterns that could render it flat and almost invisible. Eventually relocating a nightjar using landmarks it was very easy to repeatedly lose it again.

The real bonus was that one could be seen from the clearing where I had been making my studies. This would add a further dimension to the study.

It was fascinating to observe such details of this female as the tiny bill and huge gape-line bordered by long, strong stiff-looking bristles. Now, at a greater distance, she began to relax and open her eyes wider, although never fully

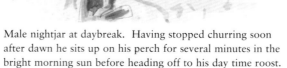

Male nightjar at daybreak. Having stopped churring soon after dawn he sits up on his perch for several minutes in the bright morning sun before heading off to his day time roost.

opening them. It was interesting to see her sitting with wings tucked under her broad flat tail further aiding camouflage. Initially the variety of markings, colours and tones seemed bewildering so to draw and paint them I found it easier to blur my eyes and let the detail merge into more regular blocks and patterns.

The following pictures form snap-shots of both behaviour and developments at the nest site as the breeding season progressed. These observations were made at intervals of several days. This was a deliberate measure for two reasons, the main one being to avoid unnecessary disturbance to the nightjars. The second was more selfish as I had a contract to survey all the breeding birds of a large area of grazing marshes further along the coast. This day-job, combined with the 'anti-social' hours of nightjar study, often meant that I arrived home after midnight. Then getting up again at 3am could be a bit excessive.

Nevertheless, these regular snap-shots do at least provide a short narrative of these particular nightjars' summer and give a little further insight into what these fascinating birds do when they are not entertaining us with their twilight shows.

The nest paintings were mostly made in the early morning hours of the long June days before most of us would normally be up and about. This was a deliberate action to avoid drawing people's attention to the nest site. They were also made unobtrusively and rapidly, with the aid of a telescope. This has the double effect of not causing unnecessary disturbance and by keeping to regularly used public paths, avoiding leaving new tracks with human scent. These can lead ground predators like foxes or stoats towards the nest sites. Happily, these nests proved successful and I like to believe that the extra care and attention helped a little towards this outcome.

Pair in courtship chase soon after dusk. 21 June 2001

Churring male, fluctuations in the pitch of the song are caused by sudden changes in head position and direction. This habit can readily be observed at dawn and dusk.

Wing clapping male. The sound is made by the wings slapping together on the upstroke.

12·06·01
Well marked ♀
late afternoon

This incubating female, aware of my presence, draws her feathers in tightly and closes her
large, dark eyes to further aid camouflage. Note her tiny bill, with large gape line, bordered
by a row of long, tough-looking, bristles. 12 June 2001

The male glides in to land on one of his favourite song perches. Before
settling he holds his wing up and leaves his broad tail fanned to show off
his pale markings. These are important visual signals in the fading light.
12 June 2001

He now begins his characteristic churring song. This beautiful song brings a whole new atmosphere of mystery in the fading light on the heath. The churring may continue over long periods, fluctuations in the song are readily noted by sideways and upward movements of the head. When directly facing you the noise can be incredibly loud at close range. Before taking flight the churr begins to slow down, this noise I likened to that produced by a fly-wheel slowing down. The bird now launches itself into flight and a series of wing-claps now ring out from in between the gorse. 12 June 2001

A relaxed female, not bothered by my presence, in early morning.
13 June 2001

The previous evening I had noted the female resting with one wing exposed and wondered whether this indicated hatching. The following morning two egg shells could be seen behind her confirming any suspicions. Surprisingly the pair made no attempts to remove the shells and they remained on view until the young fledged. 20 June 2001

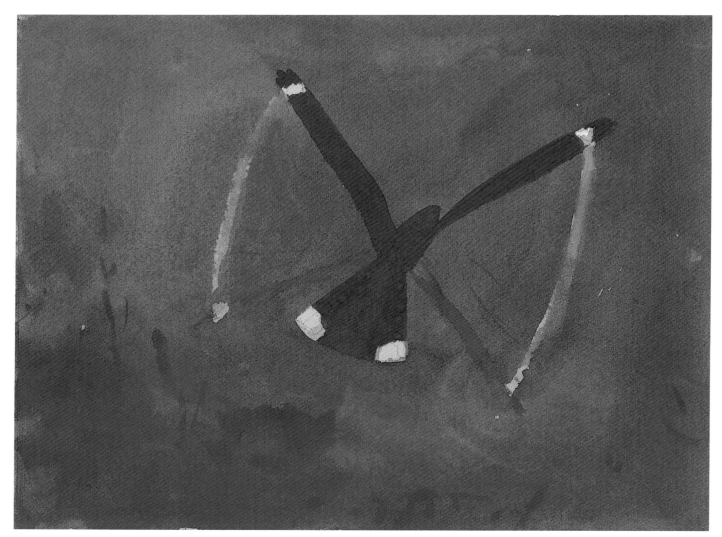

On hatching the males' behaviour in the evening changed dramatically. As I headed along the main path to my normal study area he flew in front of me in a strange flickering flight, his wingbeats slower than normal with tail fanned. On the upstroke and downstroke the wings were held static for a split second so that the white wing-patches seemed to flash. The slowed down wing-beats also produce a pale arc. This combined with the white tail spots and curious single clicks, as if from a castanet produced a striking display and I soon realised that he was trying to distract me from the immediate area, I duly obliged. 28 June 2001

Female sheltering young under her wing. 23 June 2001

Male distracting me away from nesting area by showing off his luminous tail and wing-spots to their full advantage.

The two chicks in the early morning sun. One resting under its mother's tail and the other under her wing. Later in the day the sun was very hot and the mother and her young had moved into shade. 26 June 2001

A woodcock's roding circuit passed right over my nightjar study area. Most evenings, just as the nightjars made their first churrs, he would pass over at tree top height sounding his peculiar high whispers and frog-like croaks. This evening he passed over with a second bird below and, at regular intervals, he would momentarily stall above it and fan his tail showing off his luminous white spots that woodcock share with male nightjars. Whether his companion was a mate or a rival I am unsure.

The chicks begin to show the first signs of their cryptic feathering which has begun to replace their down.
28 June 2001

Following a courtship chase the female alights on a bough and the male lands by her side.
She leans forwards submissively as if inviting mating when suddenly an additional male lands
directly in front and a wild chase follows.

This behaviour shows the females' readiness to start a second brood. The male now takes over
tending the young and the female makes a new nest. 5 July 2003

The tell-tale white patch just visible on the underside of the wing feathers showed this to now be the male who had taken over tending the young. The female, having remated, will be busy making a new nest.

3 July 2001

Male tending young. The young birds showing stumpy wing and tail feathers and in a week or so will be ready to fly. These young successfully fledged but the whereabouts of the female's second brood was unknown. I didn't even bother to search for it in the now waist-high bracken. Just to have witnessed this family growing up was more than I had hoped for. 4 July 2001

The height of summer

Back on the coast the saltmarshes are dominated by a carpet of sea lavender. Bright but overcast days, particularly in the morning and evenings are the best times to see it as the colour is most intense and appears to shimmer. 28 July 2001

Hot, sunny days of high summer frequently sees huge swarms of flying ants towering over towns and villages. Huge bundles of swifts, black-headed gulls and starlings feast on the bounty of insects. When one column is exhausted or disperses they turn to another, at which point the gulls get quite frenzied. Already at this time of year the gulls have lost their dark hoods and have begun to replace old flight feathers, these appear as symmetrical gaps in their wings. Wells Town, August 2001

The saltmarshes at Wells and Warham.
28 July 2001

On warm, sunny evenings groups of swifts gather and race over the pantiles and through gaps in between houses uttering their loud, screaming calls. Their numbers swell as more and more young fledge.
Jolly Sailor Yard, Wells – 25 July 2000

113

The numbers of swifts reach a peak in August when all the young have
left their nests. Their noisy evening manoeuvres continue to entertain
until around the middle of the month when suddenly everything is quiet
and the whole breeding population of the town or village has suddenly
left for their winter quarters in Africa.

Wighton Churchyard – 27 July 2000

Two fledgling spotted flycatchers suddenly appeared on the garden fence one morning, obviously from a nest nearby. The young wait side by side for their parents to return with food. They instinctively follow the flight paths of hoverflies moving from one hogweed blossom to another.
Kirkgate Lane, Wighton – 2 August 2001

12 Aug 96 Late pm
lots landing → fields.

Cormorant numbers often reach a peak in mid-August when large numbers gather at their nightime roosts. They have a complex visual and vocal language and their interactions are highly entertaining to watch and draw. Holkham Park – 12 August 1996

The return passage of waders

To the beginner or casual observer the identification of mixed groups of waders is so confusing and bewildering that it often leads to despair and the belief that they will never master the identification of this group of birds. I can certainly relate to this, as these were my feelings, during my early teens, when looking at a gang of mixed waders on a small section of mud to the east of Wells Quay. It all seemed straightforward in the field guides: 'look at this colour or marking' but often in life, colours and patterns may not be so obvious and every small wader looks essentially grey-brown. Then comments like 'stockier than a dunlin' are not much use to a beginner, particularly when you're not completely sure which one is a dunlin!

Stick with it; learning the identification skills required for this initially tricky group won't happen overnight. With hindsight my bewildering group of waders was a group of dunlin, knot and

Juvenile little stint

redshank. The redshank mystery was solved relatively quickly due to its obvious 'red shanks'. This identification was confirmed when it flew showing white patches on the trailing edge of the wings and a sharp white wedge pointing up its back. The process of correctly naming it was very satisfying. Then, when the observation was repeated a few days later, its appearance became more familiar, as did its noisy call and experience was slowly gained. The dunlin and knot however, took a little more time but progress was gradually made. This is how the process works.

Then, with a trip to Cley or Titchwell in late summer or early autumn, the bewildering scenes surface once more. These two places are amongst the very best sites to see waders in the British Isles and if you happen to visit them during a large passage the variety and number of species can be breathtaking.

Your new found confidence collapses; the dunlin, a recently solved mystery is now totally confusing once again with the arrival of differently marked juvenile birds and adults in various stages of moult between their breeding and winter colours. This is further compounded by the fact that there are individuals from different geographical races, which even differ slightly in their size and structure; some have long bills, others short!

A good example of how a single species can vary enormously is the ruff. Male ruffs have very elaborate breeding plumage, a mane of feathers around the head from which they take their name. Furthermore, the colour and markings vary individually; some have pure white ruffs, others white with black barring and yet others

Male ruff in winter plumage.

Turnstones sorting through bladder wrack for sandhoppers and nearby a resting
oystercatcher. I painted these as the light was rapidly fading and could still hear them
raking through the tideline long after dusk had fallen. Blakeney Point – July 1999

rusty-red and orange. The pattern and colours change from white through oranges, reds and chestnuts until we see birds with completely black ruffs. These elaborate feathers are quickly moulted after the lekking displays on northern bogs, marshes and tundra and by the time we see them again in late summer they have a confusing, moth-eaten patchwork of moulted and un-moulted feathers.

The females are considerably smaller and less showy, mainly mottled with grey, brown and black. The appearance and sizes of the sexes is so different that early ornithologists regarded them as two separate species, the males known as the ruff and the females a separate species called the reeve. These names are often still used today when referring to the sexes.

Identification is further complicated by the arrival of young birds in early autumn. They can appear fractionally smaller again than their respective parents, mainly due to their sleeker plumage. Furthermore, this plumage is different; youngsters are dressed in warmer, rich buffs and browns with neat, dark centres to their back feathers.

So, sorting out the appearance of just one species is enough to keep you occupied all day, but, as stated earlier, stick with it; things will slowly begin to fall into place.

Alarmed redshank taking flight.

Good quality optics are now affordable and there are a couple of excellent field guides to help you on your way.

As skill and confidence grow it is very satisfying to feel progress is being made. After a couple of seasons watching it is a pleasant surprise when someone asks for your help in identifying one of these 'mystery waders' and you're able confidently tell them how and why it's a dunlin.

Grey Plover

Once the basic identification skills have been mastered the enjoyment of these passage waders can be greatly enhanced by knowledge of their great migrations and higly varied breeding behaviour. One could be forgiven for thinking that because they favour similar feeding habitats as each other in Norfolk, they would nest in similar coastal habitats abroad. This is, however, far from the truth and the songs, displays, nesting behaviour and choice are incredibly wide and varied. I personally believe that, as a group, they rival the antics and displays of such famous 'showmen' as the birds of paradise. Take, for instance, the habitat choice of three familiar passage waders; sanderling, knot and green sandpiper: sanderling prefer to nest in the northern-most extremes of land, the high arctic which is unfrozen just long enough for them to make one breeding attempt. The knot will also nest on the high arctic shores but most prefer to nest on the barren tops of lonely arctic mountains. The green sandpiper on the other hand is more at home in vast, damp, Scandinavian and Russian forests where it will lay its eggs in an old song thrush or jay's nest up in the canopy.

The songs and displays are so different. We all know the dramatic aerial tumbling display of the lapwing and the peculiar drumming displays of the snipe, where the strange vibrating 'drumming' noise is produced by the air flow over its specially evolved tail feathers. Then there is the less well known aerial display of the jack snipe with its curious 'galloping horse' calls or the noisy trilling songs of Temminck's stints as they hover over their territories.

Then there is the incredible range of the different species' breeding behaviour. Greenshank behave in a manner that we may expect from nesting birds. The pair mate and stay together, taking turns to incubate their eggs and then look after their young. Spotted redshanks, on the other hand, despite being closely related, behave very differently. The female, having been courted by a male, lays a clutch of eggs.

She may stay around the nesting area for up to a week or so but it is the male alone who incubates the eggs and cares for the young. Often she will never even see her chicks, for, by this stage she will normally have long departed south.

Already in June we see the first returning females back in Norfolk having left their mates in far-off arctic bogs. At this time of year they are clad in the beautiful sooty-black breeding dress, which gives them their old, rather attractive name, dusky redshank. However, as the summer progresses, these dark feathers are replaced by pale grey and they begin to take on a mottled appearance.

Little stints' habits are different again. These waders nest across the Siberian arctic tundra. The northern summer is short so having arrived on the nesting grounds they soon mate. Their nesting habits are interesting in that the female will lay a clutch of eggs which the male will incubate and then rear the chicks by himself.

Greenshank

The female will re-mate, disperse and lay a clutch for herself, which she will rear alone. This unusual behaviour is mirrored all over their range. I have seen little stints at the nest on three occasions when these tiny birds noisily threatened me, walking around my feet with their back feathers raised and tails spread until I retreated a couple of paces. Then they returned to their nests, shuffled their bodies down into the cup, so that the eggs touched the bare flesh of the brood patches. They then continued to incubate, indifferent to me being only a few feet away.

A further and quite bizarre example of the complex and varied behaviour of waders is illustrated by the phalaropes. The female is the dominant of the sexes and has a brighter, showier breeding plumage. Females will pursue, court and fight over the drabber males. It is always a very strange moment when finally, after her persistent advances, the male gives in to her but, instead of adopting a submissive position of course he mates with her. This is always a strange moment, when one is so used to courtship displays initiated by the male.

She soon lays a clutch of eggs for him, then, feeling her part is done, she gathers with other females to form large flocks on nearby pools or on the open sea where they swim like miniature gulls, rapidly picking insects and crustaceans from the water. The male's drabber plumage is more suited to camouflage him as he incubates his eggs amongst similarly coloured dead sedges at pool edges.

Redshank

Yet more dramatic, colourful behaviour starts as the eggs begin to hatch and the young waders emerge. Many adults have special calls to tell their young to crouch and freeze if danger approaches. The delicate mottled down feathers provide incredibly good camouflage against the ground and vegetation. They have a further 'all clear' call for the young when danger has passed. However, if the approach of potential predators becomes a threat to their chicks, many species will adopt different tactics, which may include mobbing, threatening or feigning injury. In the last situation, the parents attract the attention of predators by feigning one or both broken wings; this is combined with weak and feeble looking movements and distressed calls. Predators are intended to be attracted by this seemingly injured bird and are lured further and further away from the young. Once the parent is satisfied that danger is far enough away, the pathetic-looking bird suddenly makes a full, apparently miraculous, recovery and disappears from view, creeping back to their young when danger has passed.

Young Common Sandpiper

So what makes watching passage waders in North Norfolk so fascinating for me is the journey of the imagination that they bring with them. I have been incredibly fortunate to have spent two whole summers watching breeding waders in Lapland and Siberia. There I have experienced some of their mystery, songs, display and nesting habits in a vast wilderness, with all its extremes of weather in the twenty-four hour daylight of the arctic summer.

Young curlew sandpipers, dunlin, ruff and little stint gather on the Eye Pool at Cley.
Strong north-west wind with squalls – 3 September 2001

So when watching a group of newly-arrived migrant waders feeding amicably side by side on a Norfolk coastal pool, it is incredible to think that the knot may have originated from high mountain ranges in Greenland, turnstones from high-arctic Canada, dunlin from populations in the Baltic and western Siberia, bar-tailed godwits from remote Russian bogs and little stints from nests amongst the tiny dwarf willows of the Siberian tundra.

But, for many waders, our coastline is by no means the end of their journey. North Norfolk may only be the middle phase, a port of call to stop off and feed. Curlew sandpipers may head on to spend the winter in the coastal lagoons of Namibia where they feed amongst hordes of flamingo and pelican. Whimbrels from Scandinavian bogs and forest-edges will leave the Norfolk saltings to make their way south to the mangrove swamps of West Africa where they feed amongst the fiddler crabs and mudskippers. Or how about the wood sandpipers which nest in vast, remote Scandinavian bogs and forest marshes and stop off to feed on our freshwater marshes. In a months-time they may be feeding on the edges of an African waterhole, alongside bright-coloured jacanas, where the eyes and nostrils of crocodiles protrude from the water and groups of wary zebra and antelope cautiously come in to drink.

Black-tailed Godwits

Young Redshank

124

Hidden away on the edge of tidal creeks watching and painting the
changing light and atmosphere of the still summer evenings is a perfect
antidote to the busy holiday season.
Wells – August 2001

The small size, delicate proportions and their yellow eye-rings tell these young little ringed plovers from the larger, more thick-set, cousins the ringed plover. The loose feathers of the flanks were blown out by the wind and in turn illuminated by the back lighting.

Cley – 17 August 2001

Curlew, oystercatcher and dunlin. The curlew eating small shore crabs
and the oystercatachers digging up cockles. Wells Harbour.

Grey plover, dunlins, redshank and black-headed gulls in low evening sunshine. Blakeney Harbour – 18 August 2003

Newly arrived bar-tailed godwits and dunlins liven up the mudflats with their full breeding colours. Blakeney Point – 2 August 2003

During a late afternoon low tide, redshank and turnstones search out food, while a curlew and grey plover take time out to preen their feathers.
Blakeney Point – 5 September 2003

Young dunlin and redshank feeding on the mudflats in Blakeney harbour. The redshank seek out small shells that are frequently hidden underneath blankets of enteromorpha weed, often pulling up large strands in the process. 19 August 2003

Eye Pool Cley
midday 7 Sept 01
strong NW gale
sun + cloud.

Juvenile curlew sandpipers wading up to their bellies. They duck their heads
under water to probe the silt with their long, curved bills.
Eye Pool, Cley – 7 September 2001

Whimbrel and bar-tailed godwits migrating low over
the sea. Blakeney Point – August 2003

Stiffkey high tide survey with onset of heavy showers 8 Aug 01 am

The fast-rising tide pushes these turnstone and dunlin up on to higher areas of
saltmarsh to roost amongst the samphire and last blooms of sea lavender. Amongst
the dunlin are single curlew sandpiper and sanderling. The locally bred young pied
wagtails pick off insects concentrated by the rising tide.
Stiffkey – 8 August 2001

With sudden chaos amongst the waders I was not too surprised to see this year old hobby approaching.
It was however a surprise to see it in pursuit of a kingfisher.
Arnolds Marsh – August 2002

At dusk a greenshank glides in calling to land in shallow tidal pools alongside redshank and curlew. Here it proceeds to run around feeding in its characteristic fast, jerky but elegant manner. The loud distinctive three note call shatters the calm of the still evening. The combination of this pleasing call and its attractive shape and gait make it a favourite amongst wader enthusiasts.

Wells Harbour – September 2002

Young redshank, greenshank and a young water rail feeding in shallow coastal pools. The greenshank are running around at high speed after sticklebacks and fish fry. One of the redshank, getting in the way, quickly flaps forwards. The water rail is locally bred and not long fledged.
Sea Pool, Salthouse – 24 August 2002

A lovely selection of young arctic nesting waders stopping off to feed together on a tiny pool at Cley beach car park. This group of juveniles comprises knot, bar-tailed godwit, curlew sandpiper, ruff, dunlin and little stint.

Cley Eye Pool – 2 September 2001

138

22·08·00 Ege Pool Cley Lakenning.

Young ruff, dunlin and curlew sandpipers. Although having flown thousands of miles from remote nesting grounds these birds may have only hatched five or six weeks previously. Treated with a little caution these waders can be remarkably fearless of man, indeed you may even be some of the first humans that they will have ever encountered.

22 August 2000

As the wader passage gets into full swing the first passerine migrants begin to appear in coastal scrub. Wheatears, willow warblers and whitethroats are often amongst the first to arrive. Initially it is difficult to know where these birds may have originated; they may well be part of localised movements of British-bred birds rather than the beginnings of the huge exodus from northern Europe.

The arrival of the first pied flycatcher, however, suggests a Scandinavian origin. In the east coast birdwatching calendar it signifies the end of summer and the first real day of autumn.

Here its arrival has a double significance as it also brings to an end this particular book. The following seasons are another story.

Acknowledgements

Special thanks to John Walters for producing the final layout and design of this book. The combination of his natural history knowledge and design skills have once more been invaluable.

To Natasha Drury for doing the typing, and to Roger and Margot Brownsword for commenting on the text. Also many thanks to all the family, friends and other people who have helped in numerous other ways.

Finally I am proud to have a foreword by Ian Wallace. He is probably best known for his contribution to the art of field observation and identification of birds. His articles and sketches, with their characteristic D.I.M.W. signature, spanning over four decades have been synonymous in building the foundations and development of the finer points of field observation.

However, for me, I have always been equally impressed with his more personal writing of encounters with birds, places and landscapes, and his histories of early ornithologists. There is always a great passion and enthusiasm for his subject and his book *Discovering Birds*, sadly now long out of print, perfectly sums up the pleasure and excitement of being outdoors birdwatching. The overall feel of this small book is something close to what I strive for in my own projects.

Pied flycatcher with its characteristic, split-second, wing flicking.